OWEN & MZEE

THE LANGUAGE OF FRIENDSHIP

Told by ISABELLA HATKOFF, CRAIG HATKOFF, and DR. PAULA KAHUMBU

With photographs by PETER GRESTE

SCHOLASTIC PRESS / NEW YORK

THIS BOOK IS DEDICATED TO CHILDREN ACROSS THE GLOBE WHO TOO OFTEN FACE THE UNCERTAIN, THE UNKNOWN, AND THE UNTHINKABLE, AND YET CONTINUE TO INSPIRE THE WORLD WITH THEIR RESILIENCE AND HOPE.

PRONUNCIATION GUIDE

Aldabra	al-DAH-brah
boma	BO-mah
Malindi	mah-LIN-dee
Mombasa	mom-BAH-sah
Mzee	mm-ZAY
Sabaki (River)	sah-BAH-kee
Swahili	swah-HEE-lee

Copyright © 2007 by Turtle Pond Publications LLC and Lafarge Eco Systems Ltd.

Photographs copyright © 2007, 2006, 2005 by Peter Greste. • Endpaper illustration copyright © 2006 by Isabella Hatkoff, used by permission.

Additional photographs © 2007, 2006 by: Tanya Leakey [pages 4, 14, 17, 24, 25, 26, 37]; Joe Downing [page 10]; and Paula Kahumbu [page 11]. The map in the "More About..." section by Jim McMahon.

All rights reserved. Published by Scholastic Press, an imprint of Scholastic Inc., *Publishers since 1920*. SCHOLASTIC, SCHOLASTIC PRESS, and associated logos are trademarks and/or registered trademarks of Scholastic Inc.

Library of Congress Cataloging-in-Publication Data

Hatkoff, Isabella.

Owen & Mzee: the language of friendship / told by Isabella Hatkoff, Craig Hatkoff, and Paula Kahumbu; with photographs by Peter Greste.—1st ed.   p. cm.

Sequel to: Owen and Mzee. Includes bibliographical references and index.

1. Hippopotamus-Behavior-Kenya-Juvenile literature. 2. Aldabra tortoise-Behavior-Kenya-Juvenile literature. 3. Social behavior in animals-Kenya-Juvenile literature. I. Hatkoff, Craig. II. Kahumbu, P. (Paula) III. Greste, Peter, ill. IV. Title.

QL737.U57H38 2007   599.63'5139-dc22   2006015612

ISBN-13: 978-0-439-89959-8 / ISBN-10: 0-439-89959-1

10 9 8 7 6 5 4 3 2 1   07 08 09 10 11

Printed in Singapore 46 • First edition, January 2007

Book design by Elizabeth B. Parisi • The text was set in 14.5pt. Adobe Garamond.

The authors wish to thank the Lafarge Group management, whose commitment to the environment has made this true story possible, and all of the dedicated employees of Bamburi Cement Ltd, especially Steven Tuei and his team, who take care of Owen and Mzee every day. We would also like to thank Juliana Hatkoff, who helped and inspired us to make this book.

Dear Friends,

When we first saw the now-famous picture of Owen and Mzee in the newspaper snuggling together, we were immediately inspired. But we had no idea that this single picture would lead us on a journey full of discovery, enlightenment, and many surprises across two continents. Now, a year and a half later, the inseparable pair still live and thrive together at Haller Park in Mombasa. Owen and Mzee are rarely seen more than a few feet apart as they swim, eat, sleep, and play—always together. Their bond is stronger than ever. They have even created a new language of their own, communicating with each other very clearly about their intentions and what is on their minds. Authored together by two incredibly different creatures, it is the language of friendship.

Perhaps friendship is the cement that bonds us all together. That Owen and Mzee were actually brought together at a former limestone quarry used for making cement sets the stage for a powerful metaphor. Nearly 35 years ago, the Bamburi Cement Company decided to restore the quarry into a magnificent wildlife sanctuary run by an extraordinary team of environmental conservationists. It is a place where nature is the fuel of life. What a beautiful message: When we take from the earth, we must then give back. Friendship, respect, and conservation may be the keys to saving our planet. What better spokesmen for these themes could there be than Owen and Mzee, who have already taught us so many lessons?

We hope you enjoy our second installment — Owen and Mzee: The Language of Friendship.

With love and hope,

Craig Hatkoff   Isabella

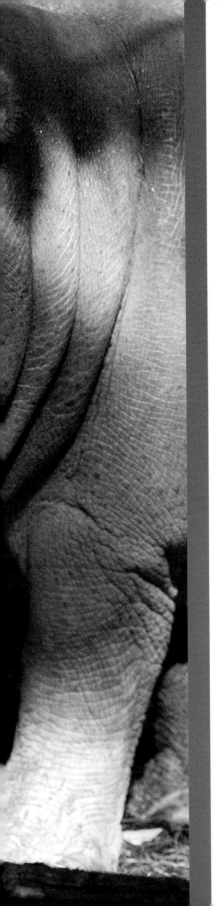

I N A SPECIAL PLACE IN KENYA live two great friends: a young hippopotamus named Owen, and a 130-year-old giant tortoise named Mzee. No one guessed that they would become friends, or that they would become famous around the world. And no one expected that their friendship would last so long. But the story of Owen and Mzee has always been full of surprises.

Here is the true story of their first remarkable year and a half together.

When Owen was a baby, he lived with his mother in a pod with about twenty other hippos. Their home was the Sabaki River in Kenya. But when Owen was about one year old, his life changed forever.

That December, the river flooded, and the hippo pod was washed down to the river mouth, near the coastal village of Malindi. That is where the hippos were on the morning of December 26, 2004, when the surging waves of a powerful tsunami struck. Afterwards, only one hippopotamus could be seen: the baby hippo who came to be known as Owen.

Hundreds of villagers and visitors worked all day to rescue Owen from the coral reef on which he was stranded. Owen was only about two feet tall, but he weighed a solid 600 pounds, and the seawater made him very slippery. Owen wasn't used to people, and out of fear and anger, he tried to escape from anyone who came near. Finally, a courageous visitor named Owen Sobien tackled the baby hippo, giving the others just enough time to secure him with a net. The joyous crowd named the hippo Owen in honor of this brave man.

Stephen Tuei from Haller Park came to Malindi to help.

Owen was stranded on a coral reef and couldn't reach the shore.

Many hours later, after a long, jolting ride in the back of a truck, Owen arrived at what would become his new home: a lush wildlife sanctuary called Haller Park, which was developed on the site of a restored limestone quarry. The park workers, including Dr. Paula Kahumbu, the manager, Sabine Baer, ecologist, and Stephen Tuei, the chief animal caretaker, thought carefully about where in the park Owen should go. Three full-grown hippos already lived at Haller Park. But hippos often attack other hippos they don't know, and young Owen might be in danger if he were placed with them. Instead, they chose an enclosure, or *boma*, where smaller, gentler animals lived: bushbucks, vervet monkeys, and a few Aldabra tortoises. One of those tortoises was a grumpy 130-year-old male named Mzee.

Mzee was always known as a loner. That was about to change.

It was late at night when Owen was finally set free into the *boma*. No one could believe what happened next. Owen scrambled straight across the clearing to Mzee and crouched down behind him. Mzee seemed annoyed and crawled away. But Owen followed. The next morning, Owen and Mzee were found snuggled up against each other. Their extraordinary friendship had begun.

At first, Dr. Paula, Sabine, and Stephen doubted that the bond between this baby hippo and giant tortoise would last. They expected Owen would soon realize that his new "parent" was not a hippo at all. And it is virtually unheard of for a reptile such as Mzee to form any attachments with another animal, especially a mammal such as Owen. But nothing turned out the way anyone expected.

During the first days after Owen's rescue, his caretakers were worried because Owen wasn't eating the leaves that Stephen left out for him. Still a nursing baby, Owen hadn't learned yet how to forage for grass. Then they noticed that Mzee seemed to be showing Owen what to do. Before long, Owen was chewing on a few leaves, too.

The bond between Owen and Mzee was almost immediate — and a surprise to everyone.

As the weeks went on, everyone watched in wonder as Owen and Mzee spent more and more time together. They wallowed in the pond together, ate together, and slept side by side. Mzee's companionship seemed to be helping Owen heal from the trauma of his difficult experiences.

News of this astonishing friendship spread quickly around the world. People flocked to Haller Park to see Owen and Mzee for themselves. Those who couldn't travel to Kenya read about them in books, in news stories, and on the Internet. Owen and Mzee were beloved stars.

Now, a year and a half later, their friendship is stronger than ever. Their bond has developed beyond what anyone has ever seen between two such different animals. To the workers who observe them every day, Owen and Mzee clearly seem to have true affection for each other. They often see Owen licking Mzee's face, or Mzee resting his head on Owen's broad belly. They seem happiest when they are together.

When Owen first arrived, he depended on Mzee for a sense of security.

The two friends share every meal.

Like any friendship, theirs has changed over time. At first, Owen was easily frightened and often scurried behind Mzee for safety. Now, Owen is a bit more independent, running through the brush on his own and splashing noisily as he flips himself around in the pond. He has also become very protective of Mzee. Owen is still deeply suspicious of people, and when workers or visitors come too close to Mzee, Owen may snort or open his jaws wide in a threatening yawn. Once, he even chased Dr. Paula and Sabine out of the *boma*.

However, though Owen is now quite a bit larger than Mzee, the old tortoise is clearly the one in charge. Owen watches Mzee closely, raising his head when Mzee raises his head, and eating what Mzee eats, when Mzee eats. Mzee sets the pace as they wander the grounds together, even though a tortoise moves much more slowly than a hippo. Owen will either plod along with Mzee, or walk ahead a few steps at his own speed and then wait for him to catch up.

Owen is bigger now, but he still lets Mzee take the lead.

**Owen is protective of Mzee.
His open mouth
means "stay away!"**

Mzee can be rather bossy. One day, when the two of them were feeding together, Owen finished eating first and he went into the pond. But it seems Mzee wanted Owen to wait. Mzee followed Owen into the pond and pushed him toward the shore until Owen got out. Then Mzee returned to his meal. When Mzee finished, Owen followed as Mzee led the way into the water.

But most of the time, Mzee, whose name in the Swahili language means "wise old man," is like a gentle guardian to Owen. When Owen is upset by people or noise and prepares to charge, Mzee often blocks Owen's way and calmly holds him off, as if reassuring Owen that there is no need for alarm. This is the kind of wise guidance that Owen's mother or father would have given him. No one knows why Mzee—a reptile, without the instincts to nurture another animal—is able and willing to nurture Owen. But clearly, he is.

Even in the water, Mzee often leads and Owen follows

They have even developed their own way of communicating. When Mzee wants Owen to walk with him, he will gently nip Owen's tail with his sharp beak. When Owen wants Mzee to move, he will nudge Mzee's feet. To direct Mzee to the right, he will nudge Mzee's back right foot. To direct him to the left, he will nudge Mzee's back left foot. If Mzee doesn't respond right away, Owen may squeeze Mzee's foot between his teeth until he starts to move. But neither ever hurts the other.

Even more remarkably, Owen and Mzee seem to have developed their own "language" of sounds. At times, one of them will make a soft, deep, rumbling sound, and then the other will repeat it. They call quietly back and forth to each other this way for hours. The sound is not one that either hippos or tortoises usually make. It seems to be an original form of communication that has grown out of their special bond. It is the "language" of their friendship.

Mzee is about to give Owen's tail a nip — time to get moving!

Dr. Kashmiri treats a crack in Mzee's shell.

Only once have Owen and Mzee spent more than a day apart, and that was for two weeks when Mzee needed veterinary treatment. A crack in Mzee's shell had become infected, and when the wildlife veterinarian, Dr. Kashmiri, tried to examine Mzee, Owen became very protective and began to charge at him. So Mzee was moved to a smaller enclosure where Dr. Kashmiri could safely treat him. For the first few days without Mzee, Owen wandered restlessly around the *boma* all alone. Then he became curious about a small Aldabra tortoise in the enclosure, Toto.

At first, Toto, whose name means "little one" in Swahili, crawled away when Owen tried to feed near her or lick her shell. But just as with Mzee, Toto soon accepted Owen's attention, and before long she was joining him for naps or walks around the *boma*. Owen and Toto had never paid much attention to each other before. But soon the two were nearly always together. Owen had made another friend.

Owen made a new friend: little Toto.

But no friend could be as special as Mzee. At last Mzee's shell healed and he was returned to the *boma*. Immediately, Owen rushed to Mzee's side. For the next several days, Owen and Mzee stayed close together, and Owen was especially protective. But Owen hadn't forgotten about his new friend Toto. Now Owen, Mzee, and Toto have become a friendly threesome, resting their heads on each other and dozing together during the heat of the day.

Hippos are playful, social animals, and seem happiest when they are part of a family group. And Owen seems very content within this most unusual family group. But Dr. Paula and the others are concerned that in many ways, Owen is behaving more like a tortoise than a two-year-old hippo. He eats what Mzee eats, rather than what hippos should eat. Though Owen can hear the bellows of the other hippos of Haller Park calling to one another, he never joins in, as if he doesn't know that he, too, is a hippo. And while hippos are usually active during the cool hours of the night, Owen is active during the day, when his tortoise friends are awake. Owen's caretakers feel that it's time for him to spend time with other hippos. But it is unlikely that an established pod of hippos would accept him.

The caretakers at Haller Park are concerned about Owen.

Fortunately, a solution may be very close at hand. One of the hippos at Haller Park, named Cleopatra ("Cleo" for short), was also rescued as an orphaned baby. Now thirteen years old and almost fully grown, she lives on her own and seems lonely for another hippopotamus to play with. Working closely with hippo experts around the world, Dr. Paula and the others are making careful plans to introduce Owen and Cleo. If they accept each other, they will be moved to a large, new *boma*, where they can live together as friends.

Ideally, Mzee will be moved along with Owen. But it's not clear whether this would be best for Mzee. Owen is already twice the size of Mzee. When Owen is full-grown in five to ten years, he will weigh about 7,000 pounds. Owen could

hurt Mzee very badly without intending to, even if Mzee's shell weren't already damaged. In fact, some of Mzee's old injuries are the result of another young hippo's boisterous play. No one wants to separate these two great friends, and Dr. Paula and the others wonder how a separation might affect Owen. Would it seem to Owen as if he were losing his family once again?

Owen gets ready for a day of play, a time when most hippos are resting.

Owen and Mzee — a friendship like no other.

If at all possible, Owen and Mzee will be kept together. Everyone hopes that Owen, Cleo, Mzee, and maybe little Toto will live happily together for many years. But only time will tell. No matter how things turn out, the story of their friendship will always remind the world that when you need a friend, one will be there for you. And that best friends come in all colors, shapes, and sizes.

And so *continues* the true story of Owen and Mzee and their enduring friendship.

KENYA

The country of Kenya sits on the equator on the eastern coast of Africa. Most Kenyans speak Swahili, as well as their own traditional, tribal language. Mzee [mm-ZAY] is a Swahili word meaning "elder," or "wise old man."

MALINDI

Malindi is a small town on the coast of the Indian Ocean. Many residents are fishermen. Malindi is known for its beautiful beaches and coral reefs, and thousands of visitors stay in its hotels. Many visitors took part in Owen's rescue. The small coastal city of Mombasa is about 50 miles south of Malindi.

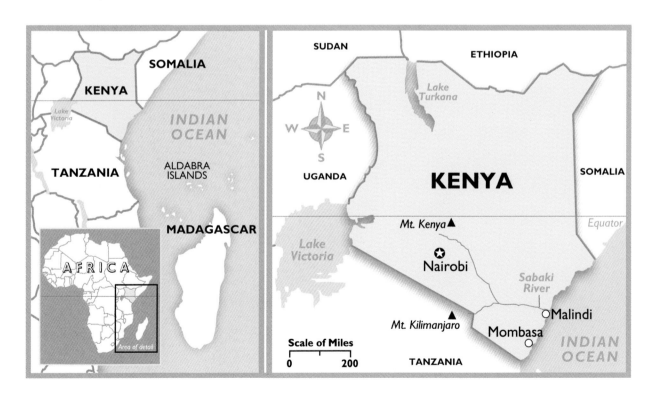

OWEN

At two years old, Owen is still a baby hippopotamus. He would have been dependent on his mother until he was about four years old. When he is full-grown, he will weigh as much as three and a half tons, or 7,000 pounds. In the wild, hippos live up to 40 years. In the safety of Haller Park, Owen may live 60 years.

Hippos live in and around rivers and lakes in much of Africa. During the day, they often lie on the riverbank, dozing in the hot sun. Their skin turns red as special glands ooze a thick liquid that protects their skin from sunburn. But most of their day is spent in the water, where they can stay cool and escape biting flies. Hippos are agile in the water, but their bodies are so dense that they aren't able to swim or float. At night, when they are more active, they roam the bush on well-worn paths, feeding on grasses, leaves, and fruit.

Hippos like to live in groups, and when young, they are very playful. But all hippos are extremely dangerous when angry or surprised, and their temper is unpredictable. Owen, along with all the wild animals at Haller Park, is much loved, but the workers know they must always be cautious around him.

Due to hunting and continual habitat loss, the hippopotamus has become an endangered species.

MZEE

Mzee is an Aldabra tortoise, the largest species of tortoise in the world, and originally from the Aldabra Islands in the Indian Ocean. Mzee is about four feet long, which is average for an adult. At around 130 years of age, Mzee is middle-aged; he could live another 70 years.

A giant Aldabra tortoise is only two and a half inches long when it hatches. Like all reptiles, it can survive on its own from its first day. An Aldabra tortoise defends itself by withdrawing into its tough, protective shell, and by using the clawlike spur on its tail, or biting with its strong, scissorlike beak. Tortoises are cold-blooded, and so are active during the day. They eat grasses, leaves, and fallen fruits, but will sometimes eat the meat of dead animals. The Aldabra tortoise is one of the few species of tortoise that is as comfortable in water as on land. It is common in zoos, but rarely reproduces there. In its original habitat, it is endangered and at risk of extinction.

Mzee came to Haller Park after being a pet for several generations of one family. Before that, no one knows how Mzee came to Africa from his birthplace. Many Aldabra tortoises were taken for food by crews of sailing ships. Perhaps he was released, or escaped during one of the frequent shipwrecks in that area. Mzee was born in the 1860s; it is amazing to consider how the world has changed during his lifetime.

HALLER PARK

Even before Owen came there to live, Haller Park was a very special place. It is named after Dr. Rene Haller, who pioneered quarry rehabilitation for Bamburi Cement Ltd. His commitment to restore the environment has transformed old limestone quarries into ecologically diverse habitats and ecosystems. Haller Park, which opened to the public 22 years ago, was his first project. Now, through Dr. Haller's methods, numerous quarries have been rehabilitated throughout the world.

Over ten years' time, barren, lifeless quarries are transformed into tropical forests. The new forests attract hundreds of kinds of animals, from antelope and butterflies to bushbabies and snakes, and other animals that have often been driven from their former habitats by human population growth.

Most of the animals at Haller Park make their own way there. But from the start, the park has been a haven for animals that were orphaned or for some reason could not be returned to the wild. Mzee was the first to come, when the family which had cared for him for several generations could no longer keep him. The hippo Cleo had been hand-raised by a family who found her orphaned in the wild when still a very young baby. When Cleo outgrew their home, they found a new home for her at Haller Park. Two other hippos were rescued from a traveling zoo in Germany.

Aside from developing and caring for this specially created environment, the workers at Haller Park are dedicated to educating people about ecology and the interdependence of animals, plants, and humans. Visit the Haller Park website (www.lafargeecosystems.com) to learn more about Haller Park and their programs and to find out how you can help.

OWEN AND MZEE AND THE TSUNAMI OF DECEMBER 2004

Owen was found stranded the day after the devastating tsunami [su-NAH-mee] that occurred in the eastern Indian Ocean on December 26, 2004. The towering waves of the tsunami were caused by a massive earthquake under the ocean floor near Indonesia. More than 175,000 people lost their lives, and whole towns were destroyed. By the time the tsunami traveled 4,000 miles to the shores of Kenya, the waves had lost much of their force, and damage there was less severe. But the whole world was shocked and saddened by the news of this disaster. The story of Owen's rescue and friendship with Mzee filled people everywhere with hope. It reminds us still that even though terrible, unpredictable things happen, the power of courage, love, and the preciousness of life will prevail.